JN025081

Integrated English for Critical Thinking

Yuya Akatsuka

SHOHAKUSHA

Acknowledgement

✦ 教科書編集にあたり、菰田真由美先生（花園大学・専任講師）、木村光宏先生（岡山理科大学・専任講師）、安田明弘先生（武蔵高等学校中学校・教諭）、平山れいさん（早稲田大学研究補助者）に様々なご協力をいただきました。

✦ 挿絵 (p. 28、p. 44) を齊藤みずきさん（早稲田大学本庄高等学院・生徒）にデザインしていただきました。

✦ 本教科書執筆の機会を与えてくださった、松柏社の永野啓子様に深く感謝申し上げます。

....

《写真》

p. 9: (Photo A) © ELSA / GETTY IMAGES NORTH AMERICA / GETTY IMAGES VIA AFP; (Photo B) © SANDY HUFFAKER / GETTY IMAGES NORTH AMERICA / GETTY IMAGES VIA AFP ✦ p. 10: © MARTIN BERNETTI / AFP ✦ p. 16: © Shawn Goldberg / Shutterstock.com ✦ p. 18: © FRANCK FIFE / AFP ✦ p. 23: © PJ_Photography / Shutterstock.com ✦ p. 31: © JOSH EDELSON / AFP ✦ p. 34: (Left) © ANTHONY WALLACE / AFP ✦ p. 35: © ALEXANDER NEMENOV / AFP ✦ p. 38: © kandl stock / Shutterstock.com ✦ p. 41: © ROSLAN RAHMAN / AFP ✦ p. 54: © HOANG DINH NAM / AFP ✦ p. 70: © MARVIN RECINOS / AFP ✦ p. 75: © VALERIE BAERISWYL / AFP

《参考資料》

✦ Vocabulary and expressions: https://dictionary.cambridge.org/ja/dictionary/english/

✦ p. 77 表: Stapleton, P. (2001). Assessing critical thinking in the writing of Japanese university students: Insights about assumptions and content familiarity. *Written Communication, 18*(4), 506–548.

はじめに

　インターネットの発達により、近年は国・地域間の体感的な距離がますます縮まってきました。例えば、地球の裏側に住んでいる人が発信した情報が、SNS等で瞬く間に共有されるようになりました。便利な世の中は一方、スマートフォン・ゲーム依存といった、国境の枠を超えた課題を浮き彫りにしました。そして、私たち人間の幸せとは何か、どのように世界がより良い場になっていくのか、といった根源的な問いをこれまでに以上に突きつけるようになりました。

　今日、英語がコミュニケーション・ツールとして多くの人たちに使用されていることに、疑いの余地はありません。複数の国・地域にまたがって課題が山積し、多くの人たちとの協同によって課題を一つひとつ解決していく必要があるのが現代社会です。その際、英語を使って考え、その考えに基づいて適切な判断をすることが求められています。そのような場面では、英語を聞いたり、読んだり、話したり、書いたりする力だけでなく、物事の本質に迫るために、様々な角度から捉え、合理的かつ客観的な視点をもちながら考える「批判的思考」が求められます。そこで、本書では、英語を聞く、読む、話す、書く、そして相手とやりとりすることを通して、総合的な英語熟達度と批判的思考の向上を目的としています。

　ところで、これまでの様々な研究によって、英語を活用する力と思考を深めることには、一定の関連性があることが立証されてきました。多くのことを英語で思考することで、これまで以上に英語を使えるようになり、自分の意見・考えを相手に伝えることができるようになります。

　本書が皆さんの批判的思考の向上と英語熟達度の向上に役立つことを願って。

2023年吉日　著者

本書の考え方

　本書は物事を様々な視点で捉えることを通して、総合的な英語熟達度と批判的思考（critical thinking）の両方を高めることを狙いとした教科書です。主な対象は、英語熟達度が欧州言語参照枠（CEFR）でA2上位〜B1レベル程度の英語学習者です。最終的にはCEFR B2上位レベルの英語熟達度に到達することを目標としています。本書の主な特徴は次の4つです。

① 豊富な語彙や表現を身につけるため、様々なテキストジャンルに触れる。
② 英語で思考する力を伸ばすため、物事を深く考える問いに出会う。
③ 英語で表現する力を高めるため、様々なテキストジャンルに対応した英文を書く。
④ オーセンティックな英文を理解し、文脈の中で文法を活用する力を高めるため、実際の使用場面を
　 意識した文構造を学ぶ。

　本書では、スピーチ原稿やブログ、電子メール、論説文といった様々なテキストジャンルに触れ、物事をじっくり考えたり、クラスメートと意見を交換するなかで考えを深めたりする活動を行います。そのために、Why? To what extent...? といった問いが多くなされます。こうした問いへの応答には、知識と語彙・表現力の両方が要求されます。Yes / Noで答えられる問いへの応答には、限られた語彙・表現力で可能ですが、答えが1つとは限らない問いへの応答には、それを表現するだけの語彙・表現力が必要です。そのため、本書では、そうした力の向上につなげるため、自己表現につながるような語彙・表現を多く入れ込んでいます。

　そして、本書には、文構造の理解を促す解説が用意されています。高等学校段階までに学習した英文法を基にしながら、英文を作成する際に役立つような情報を掲載しました。いずれの情報も、英語圏での留学あるいはアカデミックな場面等で活用できるよう、オーセンティックな内容を意識しています。加えて、本書では、英語学習者の皆さんが、スピーキングとライティングの熟達度を的確に捉え、どのようなポイントを押さえながら学習に取り組めばよいのかつかむための工夫を行っています。そのために、それぞれの技能の到達目標を示したルーブリックを用意しました。高等学校との接続を考慮して、学習指導要領（平成30年告示）で示されている資質・能力の3つの柱「知識・技能」「思考力・判断力・表現力」「主体的に学習に取り組む姿勢」を意識しつつ、教職課程のコア科目「英語コミュニケーション」の趣旨と国際バカロレアの英語科目のエッセンスを参考にしています。ライティングについては、様々なテキストジャンルの特徴を踏まえた学習ができるよう、チェックリストも用意していますので、適宜、活用いただければと思います。

▶▶▶ Contents

Rubric for Persuasive Speech

Descriptions	Knowledge and skills How well do you attend to sounds and use appropriate sentences?		Thinking, judgement, expression How well do you state your arguments and maintain coherency?[*1]	Attitude How is your presentation style?
Criterion	Sounds	Language	Message	Presentation
5-6 **Excellent**	Your pronunciation and intonation are clear and it is easy to understand what you are saying.	▸ You use vocabulary and expressions appropriate to the topic. ▸ Your sentences are understandable.	▸ You state your arguments.[*2] ▸ Your speaking is coherent.	▸ You often make eye contact with the audience. ▸ Your voice is clear.
3-4 **Acceptable**	Your pronunciation and intonation are sometimes influenced by your mother tongue, which sometimes leads misunderstandings on what you are saying.	▸ You sometimes use vocabulary and expressions appropriate to the topic. ▸ Your sentences are somewhat understandable.	▸ You state your opinions.[*3] ▸ Your speaking is somewhat coherent.	▸ You sometimes make eye contact with the audience. ▸ Your voice can be heard but is sometimes unclear.
1-2 **Developing**	Your pronunciation and intonation are strongly influenced by your mother tongue, which often leads to misunderstandings on what you are saying.	▸ You do not use vocabulary and expressions appropriate to the topic. ▸ Your sentences are difficult to understand.	You do not state your arguments or opinions, and your speaking incoherent.	▸ You make little eye contact with the audience. ▸ The voice is soft and unclear most of the time.

*1 coherency: logical and orderly and clear, follows in a natural way.
*2 arguments: claims with reason(s).
*3 opinions: statements without reason(s).

Rubric for Writing

Descriptions	Knowledge and skills How well do you write a required text type[*1] and use appropriate sentences?		Thinking, judgement, expression How well do you state your arguments and maintain coherency?
Criterion	Format	Language	Message
5-6 Excellent	You write the required text type.	▸ You use vocabulary and expressions appropriate to the task. ▸ Your sentences are understandable.[*2]	▸ You state your arguments. ▸ Your writing is coherent with no fallacies.[*3]
3-4 Acceptable	You can somewhat write the required text type.	▸ You sometimes use vocabulary and expressions appropriate to the task. ▸ Your sentences are somewhat understandable.	▸ You state your opinions. ▸ Your writing is somewhat coherent without some fallacies.
1-2 Developing	You do not write the required text type.	▸ You do not use vocabulary and expressions appropriate to the task. ▸ Your sentences are difficult to understand.	▸ You do not state your arguments or opinions, and your writing is incoherent with fallacies.

[*1] Required text type: Your writing is aligned with the type and characteristics of a text type.
[*2] Understandable: Misspellings and grammatical errors do not stand out, but you avoid significant errors; evaluate whether your English can be used to communicate with others.
[*3] fallacy: an error in reasoning

Describe a Photo

Describing a photo is an essential skill to improve your imagination and speaking skills. You can strengthen your oral compositions by doing this activity because each photo describes what something looks like – a person or a scene presenting a real situation. You can learn a lot of vocabulary and how to use expressions related to everyday life. Below are some tips on how to describe a photo.

▶ **Introduction:** Describe major information about the photo.

- This photo was taken {by/in} e.g. This photo was taken outside/in an office.
- The photo describes {WHAT} e.g. The photo describes a wedding party.

▶**Detailed information:** Divide a photo into five to nine pieces and give detailed information using an expression of 'place'.

Five pieces

	At the top	
On the left	In the middle	On the right
	At the bottom	

Nine pieces

At the top left	At the top middle	At the top right
On the middle left	In the middle	On the middle right
At the bottom left	At the bottom middle	At the bottom right

You can also use: 'behind', 'in front of', 'next to', 'above', 'between A and B', and 'in the background' etc.

Point 1

Use the present continuous tense (be + V-ing) when describing a person.
i.e., A man standing on the left is reading a newspaper.

Point 2

Keep an objective viewpoint.

✗   A person standing in the middle wears <u>a beautiful watch</u> on his right hand.

The term 'beautiful' is a subjective adjective, and everyone may have a different opinion.

✓   A person standing in the middle wears <u>a watch with a brown leather strap</u> on his right hand.

Be specific and describe an objective viewpoint.

Point 3

If you do not know much about a picture, you can use the following expressions:

- The person seems…
- Maybe…
- I think…
- It seems to describe…

Now describe the photos!

A

B

Identities

はじめに

本書は、答えが１つとは限らない問いに答えながら、英語で読むこと、話すこと、書くことの力を身につけることを目的としています。そのために、まずは一人で考えてみて、次にペアを組んで意見を交換し、クラスの仲間に自分の意見・考えを伝える、という活動を行っていきます。答えがすぐに思いつかない問いもいくつかあるかと思いますが、「思考を鍛えるためのトレーニング」と思って気楽に取り組んでみましょう。

The aims of this part:

1) To explore the concept of 'identity' and imagine having a better life.

2) To enrich* your vocabulary and use of expressions relating to the concept of 'identity' by reading speech scripts.

3) To write a persuasive speech script with an understanding of the components of a persuasive speech.

* enrich 強化する

Men make a selfie as they celebrate after the passing of a bill to legalize same-sex marriage in Chile.

Look at the photo and the caption.* What came to your mind when you first saw this picture?

*caption 見出し

1.1 | Who I really am

▶▶▶Guiding questions

1. What is the meaning of **identity**? Define it using your own words. If you are not sure how to define the word, write down what comes to your mind when you hear it.

_____

_____

2. When communicating with someone, what is more important to you—relying on your emotions or thinking logically? Why?

_____

_____

_____

Introduction

When you introduce yourself, what do you say to others? You may say your name, where you are from, what you love and so on... You may also introduce your social position such as, 'I am an XX university student' 'I am a staff of such and such...' In other words, you have partially*¹ figured out who you are already. This understanding of self is called 'identity'. But in fact, the concept of 'identity' is unclear because we cannot 'see' it and may not really understand who you really are. Recent researchers are trying to define*² its concept and discussions are on-going. In this unit, the concept of 'identity' will be explored by reading speech texts and imagining having a better life.

*¹ partially 部分的に
*² define 定義づける

▶▶▶Warm-up

Understanding what you are like is a very challenging task. It is not easy to describe 'my identity is [such and such]'. 'Identity' is a set of your attributes*, beliefs, desires, or principles of action that you think in your mind. Now, make a list of your 'identity' with the figure below.

*attribute: a characteristic that we have

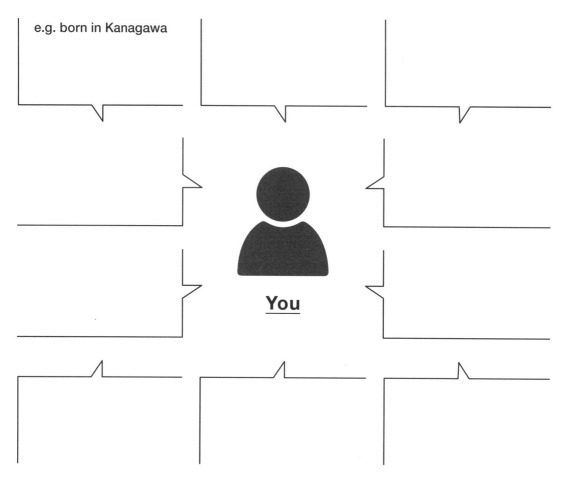

e.g. born in Kanagawa

You

Then, we describe your identity with sentences and share them with your classmates. Please note that you should not make judgements about your classmates' opinions or worldviews. Everyone's beliefs, views, and lived experiences are different.

Example: I am the youngest of three kids. I believe caring for others is the most important thing. And…

▶▶▶Writing

The concept of identity was established* in the 1950s by an American researcher, and the term refers to who you really are. Can you describe yourselves? Which group do you belong to, and what are the things you value the most? Write a short passage (not more than 50 words) based on what you learnt in the warm-up.   *establish 確立する

_____

_____

_____

_____

_____

_____

Then, share your writing with your classmates.

What is critical thinking, and why is it important?

Critical thinking is a rational,*1 multidimensional, reflective, and objective way of thinking that is an intrinsic*2 part of life. This way of thinking has become paramount*3 to live well in our society. Today, there are a variety of global issues, such as climate change, food security, and gender-related problems. To address them, we should collaborate with people worldwide through critical thinking. To this end, English is a useful tool for communication.

*1 rational 合理的な   *2 intrinsic 本質的な   *3 paramount 最重要の

1.2 | Identity spectrum

▶▶▶ Evaluate how much you know

1. Does your university take any action protecting LGBTQI+ youth? This may include actions such as providing gender-free toilets or avoiding the use of Mr/Ms/Mrs. when teachers refer to students.

_____

_____

2. If one's assigned sex at birth is male but one identifies as a woman, would a woman's university permit that person to enrol there in your country?

_____

▶▶▶ Text   🔊 Audio 02

Read a speech script about LGBTQI+ and answer the following questions.

Thank you for inviting me here. I am glad to speak with such well-aware[*1] university students. As you know, there are hundreds of people whose gender identities are different, who have a sense of feeling different from their assigned sex.[*2] I have met such people throughout my life. I am also one of them, and I

5 had been struggling to accept my gender identity for a long time. But I have found how to ensure my well-being in this modern society. Today, I would like to discuss how we can accept our gender identity and ensure our well-being.

Have you ever heard the term 'LGBTQI+'? This is an **acronym** for Lesbian, Gay, Bisexual, **Transgender**, Queer or Questioning, Intersex, and others. The

10 term is widely found on **social media** and is used to describe one's sexual orientation[*3] or gender identity. (A) I am sure most of you have heard the term. Can you imagine how difficult it is for them to ensure their well-being in their daily lives ? Before knowing the term LGBTQI+, I could not understand how I was capable of loving both men and women, even though my assigned sex was

15 female. I had suffered from a gender identity crisis. (B) It is certain that every member of the LGBTQI+ community is suffering.

It was at the session held by the Diversity Centre of the University in 2018 that I first came to know that approximately 4.4% of the people aged between 16 and

24 in the United Kingdom identified as LGB. I was surprised by this substantial*4 number. I also gained confidence that I was not alone, and gradually accepted 20 my gender identity gap. Before that session, I had believed that I should behave like a woman, get married to a man, and hide my real emotions from others. But now, I have changed my attitude and mindset and can freely choose a partner whom I really love.

Fortunately, society has gradually gained more respect for people's diverse 25 identities, and the media is interested in the issues concerning the LGBTQI+ community. My close friends try to understand and accept what I think and feel. (C) I feel very comfortable with my friends and appreciate their concern. Returning to the first question, 'How can we ensure our well-being in this modern society?', I can do so by accepting my **authentic self**. I love myself and 30 I thank God and my parents for giving me an opportunity to deeply explore everything about myself.

I know it is not easy to accept everything about yourself and who you really are. But I know God loves me, my parents accept me, and my close friends really understand me. I really want to say that the most important tip for well-being 35 is to accept yourself as you are. Thank you for listening.

*1 well-aware（状況等について）よくわかっている　　*2 assigned sex 生まれもった性別
*3 sexual orientation 性的指向　*4 substantial （数量・程度などが）かなりの

▶▶▶ Vocabulary and expressions

Numbered 1-4 below is a list of words taken from Text. Match these words with their definitions from 'a' to 'd'.

1. acronym 2. transgender 3. social media 4. authentic self	a. websites and software programmes used for social networking b. use to describe someone who feels that they are not the same gender as the gender they were said to have when they were born c. someone who isn't afraid to be true to who they are d. a word created from the first letters of each word in phrases or a sentences of words

1. (　　)　　2. (　　)　　3. (　　)　　4. (　　)

▶▶▶ Comprehension questions

If the sentences below are correct, put 'T' for True, and if incorrect, put 'F' for False. Justify your answers only for the ones which are false (no need to justify if true).

> Example: The author's assigned sex at birth was female. (T)
>
> Justification: _____ ✗ _____

1. The target audience of this speech is university students. (   )

   Justification: _____

2. The main message of this speech was to encourage* the audience to come out to others about their gender identity. (   )   *encourage 促す

   Justification: _____

3. The Q for LGBTQI+ is an acronym for queer or questioning. (   )

   Justification: _____

4. The speaker still suffers from her gender identity and is unable to accept herself. (   )

   Justification: _____

5. Approximately 4.4 percent of all UK residents* were identified as being LGB. (   )

   *resident 居住者

   Justification: _____

▶▶▶ Discussions

Answer the questions below.

1. One sentence does not follow the logical structure of the Text. Please choose one of the sentences, labelled (A), (B), or (C), and indicate* which sentence does not logically follow.
   (   )   *indicate 示す

2. In lines 19-20, the author writes, 'I was surprised by this substantial number'.
   Do you also think 'substantial'? Why?

   _____

   _____

   _____

3. In lines 23–24, the author claims, 'I have changed my attitude and mindset and can freely choose a partner whom I really love'. Even if they can chose their parners, some people do not believe that same-sex marriage should not be recognised by law. What would those who do not believe that same-sex marriage should be legal say?

   _____

   _____

   _____

   _____

4. Share your answers above with your classmates. What are your classmates' opinions about this matter?

1.3 | Roles of emotions

Randal Kolo Muani, a French footballer, argues with Mexico's goalkeeper Guillermo Ochoa after being fouled during the Tokyo 2020 Olympic Games.

1. Look at the photo and caption. Is showing an aggressive attitude as shown in the picture acceptable? If you became angry during the match, would you act as he did?

2. Read statements A and B below. To what extent do you agree with the statements? Why?

   A: Arguing with an aggressive attitude with a judge is not acceptable. It is an immature*1 act and moreover, the situation may not dramatically change even if he protests. He should stay calm.

   B: Complaining before a judge is justifiable*2 for all players. If I were a player and the judgement seemed false or unfair, I would behave in the same way.

   *1 immature 未熟な   *2 justifiable 正当と認められる

3. Share your thoughts with your classmates.

Introduction

How many of us believe that expressing our emotions to others is important? Some young adults believe that expressing emotions directly to others is not a good choice, in favour of keeping calm and thinking logically. However, can we really claim that these attitudes are better than showing emotions to others? If so, why?

Some religious leaders[1] and psychologists[2] claim that noticing our emotions is very important for living well and forming better relationships with others. For instance, when we pretend not to notice, hide, or ignore our own negative emotions, such as fear and sadness, we may build up stress in our mind. When we share what we feel with our peers, they may open their minds when communicating with us.

In this unit, the roles that our emotions play will be explored from the perspective of well-being[3] and building relationships with others.

[1] religious leader 宗教的リーダー　　[2] psychologist 心理学者
[3] well-being 「ウェルビーイング」＝健康で安心で満足できる生活状態を指す概念

▶▶▶ Warm-up

1. How often do you hide your emotions from your family members?
   a. always　　b. often　　c. sometimes　　d. rarely

2. How often do you hide your emotions from your friends?
   a. always　　b. often　　c. sometimes　　d. rarely

3. Do you think that showing your emotions is good for building relationships with your friends? Do you have any examples of this?

   _____

   _____

4. After answering these questions, we will share your answers with your classmates. How are your classmates' beliefs similar to or different from those of yours?

Read a speech script and answer the following questions.

I am Emma, a student in the Department of **Liberal Arts**. I'm not a researcher, a scientist, or a **psychologist**, so I can't discuss emotions from a scientific perspective,*1 but I'd like to talk to you based on my personal experiences as a student and what I learned at university. Today, I'd like to talk about the

5 importance of noticing our emotions to help build good relations with others.

Let me ask you: Have you ever **compared** something with others, like your grades or your pay at your part-time job? How did you feel then? Some of you might have experienced a feeling of superiority*2 when you knew that your grades were better than your friends'. Or, some of you might have felt guilty

10 when you heard that your friend's salary was lower than yours. I learned in psychology class that these spontaneous*3 reactions are called 'the social brain'. Our lecturer, Ms. Yoshida, explained the theory that all of us control our instinctive*4 emotions by imagining others' emotions. Looking back to when I was in senior high school, I always cared too much about what others thought

15 and thought negatively about myself. In other words, I was jealous and felt **overwhelmed**.

In her lecture, Ms. Yoshida introduced how we can deal with negative emotions. First, you can brush up your skills to be in a better position than others. Second, don't compare yourselves with others. Which actions are best suited for you?

20 I believe that a combination of these two actions is ideal for our well-being. The first is very **productive**, and I want to be like this. The second is also important; all of us are different and doing this may reduce our stress levels. I understand that noticing our emotions and acting in appropriate ways are not easy for us, but I believe that if we can do this, it will **contribute** not only **to**

25 forming better relationships with others but also to living well as a university student.

In conclusion, I believe that everyone is eager to create good relationships with others—your family members, your classmates, your friends, and your colleagues*5 at your workplace. As a first step to living well as a university

30 student, I urge you to notice your emotions and accept them, then brush up on your skills and don't compare yourself too much with others since everyone is different. Thank you for your attention.

*1 perspective 視点　　*2 superiority 優位性　　*3 spontaneous 自然発生する

*4 instinctive 本能的な　　*5 colleague 同僚

▶▶▶ While you are reading Text

Consider sentences 1-5 from Text. Write '**F**' if the sentence is presented as fact, and write '**O**' if it is presented as the author's opinion.

	Sentences	Fact (F) or Opinion (O)
1	these spontaneous reactions are called 'social brain'. (ll. 11)	
2	all of us control our instinctive emotions by imagining others' emotions. (ll. 12-13)	
3	all of us are different and doing this may reduce our stress levels. (l. 22)	
4	I believe that if we can do this, it will contribute not only to forming better relationships with others but also to living well as a university student. (ll. 24-26)	
5	I believe that everyone is eager to create good relationships with others (ll. 27-28)	

▶▶▶ Vocabulary and expressions

Numbered 1-6 below is a list of words taken from Text. Match these words with their definitions from 'a' to 'f'.

1. liberal arts	a. someone who studies the mind and emotions and their relationship to behaviour
2. psychologist	
3. compare	b. to examine or look for the difference between two or more things
4. overwhelm	c. to help to cause an event or situation
5. productive	d. to be too much to deal with
6. contribute to sth	e. having positive results
	f. college or university subjects, including history, languages, and literature, that are not technical

1. (   )   2. (   )   3. (   )   4. (   )   5. (   )   6. (   )

▶▶▶ Comprehension questions

1. What is the main purpose of this speech?
   a. The speaker sharing her personal experience
   b. Teaching a lecture on psychology
   c. Persuading the audience regarding the importance of noticing our emotions

2. How do we control our instinctive emotions according to the speech script?
   a. By monitoring our emotions
   b. By imagining others' emotions
   c. By caring about others' actions

▶▶▶ Discussions

1. In paragraph 3, Emma claims*1 that 'I believe that a combination of these two actions is ideal for our well-being'.

   Question: To what extent do you agree with her claim? Use a percentage to convey*2 how much you agree (0–100%). Explain why and provide reasons to support your opinion.

   *1 claim 主張する   *2 convey 伝える

   _____

   _____

   _____

2. Some students may believe that negative emotions such as jealousy and irritation* do not represent a good attitude. But is this true? Some experts say that having negative emotions is not a problem in itself. However, if we act according to our negative emotions, it will be ethically problematic, as our actions may greatly influence our relationships with others. For example, if friends do not immediately respond to text messages, they may become irritated or concerned. Feeling these emotions is a natural reaction of young adults. However, if you blame your friend based on spontaneous emotions, your friend may perceive it as bad behaviour and thus feel hurt.

   Question: To what extent do you agree with this statement? Use a percentage to convey how much you agree (0–100%). Explain why and provide reasons to support your opinion.

   *irritation いら立ち

   _____

   _____

   _____

3. After answering the above-mentioned questions, you will share your answers with your classmates. How are your classmates' beliefs similar to or different from those of yours?

1.4 | Subculture

1. Look at the photo. What came to your mind when you first saw this picture?
2. Make a caption of this picture. After that, read your caption to your partner.
   Caption (   )

▶▶▶ Guiding questions

1. What comes to your mind when you hear the word 'subculture'?

_____

_____

_____

2. To what extent do you think 'subculture' relates to our identities?

_____

_____

_____

3. The concept of culture can mainly be divided into two (major culture and subculture), but how can we distinguish between them? Can we clearly differentiate these two cultures?

_____

_____

_____

Introduction

Have you thought about what a subculture is? In Japan, kabuki, judo, and origami are thought to be part of the traditional culture. These types of culture can be called 'major culture', because most people have recognised them. Contrarily, anime and B-kyu Gourmet are categorised as 'subculture', because these are new, and have yet to be shared by the majority.

The concept of subculture first came up in the late 1970s in Anglophone countries,* such as the UK and the US. For example, hip-hop, rap music and skateboarding are categorised as subcultures. In modern society, the concept of subculture is accepted and recognised by a variety of ages and genders worldwide.

This section explores the concept of subculture by focusing on a campaign for promoting inbound tourism in Japan.

*Anglophone countries 英語圏の国

▶▶▶Warm-up

Before starting a more in-depth* exploration of subculture, we examine the words listed below

*in-depth 掘り下げた

Related words of 'subculture'
slang, fashion, music, clothing, gender, otaku (people obsessed with anime and manga), youth culture, Akihabara, kawaii, cosplay, gaming, hip-hop, skater, etc…

Question: Why are these words linked to 'subculture'?

_____

_____

Text

Read a following text about subculture and answer the questions.

Hello, everyone. Have you ever read articles on inbound tourism in Japan? Have you ever heard about a policy for Japanese inbound tourism? According to the Ministry of Foreign Affairs of Japan, approximately 31 million people visited Japan in 2018, which is three times the number of foreign visitors in 2013. Although these data were collected before the COVID-19 pandemic, why did the number of international tourists triple these five years? What attracted international tourists before the pandemic? Why did they choose Japan as their travel destination? What do they want to see and experience in Japan? I intend to answer these four questions and suggest ways to assist international tourists in their quest for information if the COVID-19 outbreak is mitigated.[1]

First, I will focus on the reasons for the increase in the number of foreign visitors to Japan. Experts claim that various factors, such as relaxed visa regulations and a decrease in flying costs, have contributed to this increase. I believe that the Japanese government's 'Visit Japan Campaign' is one of the major factors behind this increase in foreign visitors. This campaign promoted Japanese subcultures such as anime and fashion as 'Cool Japan',[2] and it is believed that many foreigners are attracted to these subcultures. For example, when I visited a junior college in Singapore last year, many students expressed their interest in Japanese subcultures, especially anime and B-kyu Gourmet (a variety of reasonably priced casual food), and were eager to visit Japan.

Second, I will examine the factors that attract foreign visitors and the reasons for choosing Japan as a travel destination. To this end, I conducted a survey in Asakusa and asked 89 foreign visitors about the sources they referred to while deciding their travel destinations. I found that they used social media such as Twitter and Instagram rather than paper-based booklets. Some of the family groups from Taiwan answered that they read about Asakusa on Instagram and decided to visit to enjoy sukiyaki. The survey also shows that foreign visitors are attracted to Japanese culture, which is both traditional and modern, as well as rich and colourful cuisines such as sushi, tempura, and okonomiyaki. I also found that teenagers were interested in Kawaii culture – cute fashion icons and products – which is best experienced in Harajuku, Tokyo.

Third, what do foreign visitors want to see and experience in Japan? I know that each of them has a different answer. Some want to ski or enjoy hot springs,

while others want to wear anime costumes, go shopping, or visit a film location.
35 Data show that approximately 80% of foreign visitors are from Asian countries and regions, with approximately 50% from China and South Korea. Some experts say that most Asian people want to enjoy Japanese food culture and stroll in the downtown areas.

In summary, foreign visitors expect to enjoy the diverse cultures and subcultures
40 of Japan when they visit the country. To provide them with a comfortable environment, I believe that we need a variety of support systems, such as multilingual helplines, to share information about how to take a public bath. Being a student, I would like to actively support foreign visitors by communicating with them in English, for example, by giving them directions to reach their
45 destination. If you have other ideas, please let me know and support them. Thank you for your consideration of our manuscript.

*1 mitigate やわらぐ
*2 Cool Japan is a concept adopted by the Japanese government, which promotes campaigns for foreigners or foreign visitors to recognise and experience Japanese "cool" culture, especially Japanese subculture.

▶▶▶ Comprehension questions

1. From the author's survey in Asakusa, what was inferred about foreign visitors when deciding on their travel destinations?

   a. They check whether the government had relaxed visa regulations.
   b. They explore a web site.
   c. They read a paper-based booklet.
   d. They judge whether rich and colourful cuisines are found in Asakusa.

2. What is the main purpose of the text?

   a. To introduce what the speaker found in Singapore.
   b. To encourage readers to use social media for their tours.
   c. To let readers know people from Asia tend to enjoy food culture and love to visit downtown areas.
   d. To analyse the reasons that the number of tourists increased and suggest how we can support tourists.

▶▶▶ Discussions

Work in pairs. Pick two or three topics from below and discuss with your partner.

1. Before the COVID-19 pandemic, many foreign visitors had been travelling to Japan. Data show that approximately 80% of the visitors were from Asian countries and regions, with approximately 50% from China and South Korea. If you welcome a South Korean or Chinese visitor to Osaka, Tokyo, or your local hometown, which spots would you recommend visiting?

2. Many teenagers use social media, such as Twitter and Instagram, to search for information on travel destinations. If you could promote one Japanese sightseeing spot through social media, which place would you recommend to foreigners to experience Japanese subculture?

3. Many foreign visitors enjoy Japanese food culture. In Japan, there are a variety of reasonably priced casual foods such as curry rice, ramen, and pan-fried noodles. Called 'B-kyu Gourmet', this food is regarded as one of the Japanese subcultures. Which B-kyu Gourmet would you recommend to foreign visitors?

1.5 | Writing a speech script

Introduction

How many times do we 'think' in a day? We may think 'What will I have for today's lunch', 'When is the due date of my assignment?' Indeed, we have numerous thoughts daily. According to some studies, we think approximately 10,000 times or more per day!

Here is a question. How well do you understand what others are thinking about? It is challenging to figure this out, even if they are your close friends or family members. To understand others' thoughts is a difficult task. Some of you may have been frustrated previously because your thoughts and ideas had not been understood by others. So, being able to express your thoughts clearly and delivering them with an appropriate tone and expression are important social skills.

In your academic life and at your future job, you will give a variety of speeches at meetings, conferences, or parties. You will need to deliver your thoughts in an appropriate manner depending on its purpose, as well as the targeted audience. Since speech styles vary, some knowledge of techniques is required to deliver a compelling* speech.

There are two types of speech styles: informative and persuasive. The former seeks to provide clear information to the audience, while the latter seeks to persuade them through reasonable arguments and coherence. In this section, we will look at how to deliver an effective persuasive speech.

*compelling 説得力のある

▶▶▶ Warm-up

1. What are the characteristics of a **good** speech? List what you believe to be the **three** most important characteristics:

   1) _____

   2) _____

   3) _____

2. Which of the following statements are true or false about persuasive speech?

   a. a speech starts with a clear purpose (   )

   b. a speaker does not show his/her emotions at all (   )

   c. a speech refers to facts to support a speaker's claim (   )

   d. a speech avoids referring to a speaker's personal experiences (   )

e. a speech includes terminology or jargons to show how smart a speaker is (   )

f. a speaker asks the audience a question without giving a possible answer (   )

g. a speaker encourages the audience to draw an image in their minds (   )

3. Share your answers for 1 and 2 with your classmates.

▶▶▶ How to write a speech script?

What is a good speech? How can we persuade others? What skills can we use to influence others' minds? It is recommended that speech in English be appealing, trustworthy, logical, and emotional. Ancient Greek philosopher Aristotle (384-322BC) recommended the following techniques: **ethos** (establishing your credentials), **logos** (appealing to logic), and **pathos** (appealing to emotion). These techniques are still used in modern English speech. Although some may believe that it is best to avoid using emotions to persuade others, expressing emotions is a critical factor for persuasive speech, as human beings make judgements based on their emotions. Below are examples of sentences describing ethos, logos, and pathos.

Ethos   Establishing your credentials for the audience regarding a specific subject matter, as your audience needs to know whether you are trustworthy.

e.g. I have been a dedicated junior high school teacher for 15 years, and I have found some tendencies in children's characteristics.

Logos   Persuading an audience using reason, demonstrating evidence such as facts and figures.

e.g. According to the Ministry of Education (2020), about 8% of university students suffer from game addiction.

Pathos   Showing your emotions. Your logical argument will be more persuasive when you express your emotions in your speech.

e.g. I was really happy when my students passed the entrance examination.

Now, put the names of rhetorical devices that can be categorised under ethos, logos, and pathos.

Thank you for inviting me here. I am glad to speak with such well-aware university students. As you know, there are hundreds of people whose gender identities are different, who have a sense of feeling different from their assigned sex. I have met such people throughout my life. I am also one of them [   ], and I had been struggling to accept my gender identity for a long time. But I have found how to ensure my well-being in this modern society. Today, I would like to discuss how we can accept our gender identity and ensure our well-being.

Have you ever heard the term 'LGBTQI+'? This is an acronym for Lesbian, Gay, Bisexual, Transgender, Queer or Questioning, Intersex, and others. The term is widely found on social media and is used to describe one's sexual orientation or gender identity. I am sure most of you have heard the term. Can you imagine how difficult it is for them to ensure their well-being in their daily lives? Before knowing the term LGBTQI+, I could not understand how I was capable of loving both men and women, even though my assigned sex was female. I had suffered from a gender identity crisis.

It was at the session held by the Diversity Centre of the University in 2018 that I first came to know that approximately 4.4% of the people aged between 16 and 24 in the United Kingdom identified as LGB [   ]. I was surprised by this substantial number. I also gained confidence that I was not alone, and gradually accepted my gender identity gap. Before that session, I had believed that I should behave like a woman, get married to a man, and hide my real emotions from others. But now, I have changed my attitude and mindset and can freely choose a partner whom I really love.

Fortunately, society has gradually gained more respect for people's diverse identities, and the media is interested in the issues concerning the LGBTQI+ community. My close friends try to understand and accept what I think and feel. I feel very comfortable with my friends and appreciate their concern. Returning to the first question, 'How can we ensure our well-being in this modern society?', I can do so by accepting my authentic self—who I really am. I love myself and I thank God and my parents for giving me an opportunity to deeply explore everything about myself [   ].

I know it is not easy to accept everything about yourself and who you really are. But I know God loves me, my parents accept me, and my close friends really understand me. I really want to say that the most important tip for well-being is to accept yourself as you are. Thank you for listening.

▶▶▶ Other tips for writing a speech script

It is important to know how to create speech scripts. Its purpose is to inform listeners or persuade them from their point of view. Read the text above and think about which tips can be found below in the text? The corresponding sentence(s) should be extracted from the text above.

1. Organise your thesis statement clearly and effectively.

_____

_____

2. Answer questions in your speech.

_____

_____

3. Show some evidence (e.g. data, references) to support your opinion.

_____

_____

4. The conclusion should be related to the thesis statement.

_____

_____

▶▶▶ Creating a speech script

Read the question below and create a mini-speech script in more than 150 words. Then, share it with your classmates.

The concept of subculture is sometimes associated with a negative image. For example, skateboarding can be considered a sport for bad boys or girls because it is loud, a nuisance for pedestrians, etc. However, skateboarding became an official Olympic sport with the 2020 Tokyo Olympic Games, and its status improved. How can we encourage people to form a positive image of a subculture?

Hints for writing:

1) Why do some people associate themselves with a negative image?
2) How can we minimize the negative image of a subculture?
3) How can we promote the positive image of a subculture?
4) To what extent do government agencies act to promote a positive image of a subculture?

▶▶▶ Grammar for writing

Sometimes, you can use an em dash (—) instead of a colon (:).
▶ **How to use an em dash (—)**
An em dash (—) can substitute a colon that is used to separate extra information at the end of a sentence. The em dash sets off a word or clause and adds emphasis to or expands the idea.
For example, Tom has been waiting his whole life for this moment—he is graduating from law school.

Two complete sentences should not be combined with a comma

A complete sentence that can stand on its own is called an 'independent clause'. For example, 'I completed my assignment' and 'I have not submitted it' are two independent clauses. Independent clauses cannot be separated with a comma, as this leads to a grammatical error called a 'comma splice'.

Here is an example of a comma splice:
Incorrect: 'I completed my assignment, I have not submitted it'.

To rectify* this error, the sentences should be separated by a semicolon, a period, or a comma followed by a conjunction (and, but, or, nor, for, so, yet, etc.).

Correct: 'I completed my assignment; I have not submitted it'.
Also correct: 'I completed my assignment. I have not submitted it'.
Also correct: 'I completed my assignment, but I have not submitted it'.

*rectify 修正する

▶▶▶ Reflection

1. What are the characteristics of a *good* speech? List what you now believe to be the *three* most important characteristics:

   1) _____

   2) _____

   3) _____

2. What is the meaning of '*identity*'? Define it using your own words.

   _____

   _____

3. When communicating with someone, what is more important to you—relying on your emotions or thinking logically? Why?

   _____

   _____

   _____

4. Compare these answers to your answers from pages 11 and 28. How have your beliefs changed through lessons?

Part 2

Well-being

A

B

1. Consider Photo A. Make a caption of this picture and complete the sentences below. After that, read your caption and sentence to your partner:

   Caption (   )

   This picture was taken _____ (when / where).

   A man on the left is wearing a mask and face shield because

   _____ (what).

   Behind the window, the man in the middle uses a tablet device for

   _____ (what).

2. Look at Photo B. What are they doing? Would you want to be like him or her? Why?

   _____.

3. Read the statement below. How much do you agree with it? Why?
   'The couple in photo 'B' seems to be very relaxed and are enjoying their free time. I believe that if we are rich, we could be happy like them; however, if we are poor, we cannot be happy.

   _____

   _____

   _____

The aims of this part:

1) Explore the concept of well-being and how it is accepted and applied to society.
2) Enrich your vocabulary and use of expressions relating to the concept of well-being by reading blog entries.
3) Create a persuasive blog entry with an understanding of the components of a blog that attracts readers.

2.1 | Having me time

Russian child blogger Liza Anokhina (L), 12, participates in a shoot for her blog in a Moscow park. Liza Anokhina is one of Russia's most popular child bloggers with 2.3 million followers on Instagram.

1. Look at the photo and the caption. Can you guess why Liza has been succeeding as a blogger?

2. Make a list of the three major ways to attract readers to your blog.

    1) _____

    2) _____

    3) _____

3. Compare your answers with those of your partner.

▶▶▶ Guiding questions

1. What does the term 'well-being' mean?

2. How important is it for young adults to maintain their well-being?

3. How can we improve our well-being?

Introduction

When are you happiest? Some people may feel happy when chatting with a close friend, while others may feel good while enjoying a cup of coffee in the morning. The concept of 'well-being' however, slightly differs from 'a happy moment'. A 'happy moment' is relatively short-lived, while 'well-being' lasts for a long period. In other words, well-being is sustainable, and indicates that one's physical (body) and mental (mind) health are in good condition. The concept of well-being is closely linked with health, academic, and family-related matters.

In this unit, we will be exploring the concept of well-being and how it can be applied to our society.

▶▶▶ Warm-up

1. Which exercise(s) do you want to try out to maintain your physical health?
   [multiple answers allowed]
   a. swimming   b. jogging   c. cycling   d. walking   e. other (   )

2. What practices do you want to adopt to improve your mental health?
   [multiple answers allowed]
   a. putting your smartphone away for a while
   b. maintaining a daily exercise routine
   c. having breakfast everyday
   d. chatting with family or friends
   e. other (   )

3. What helps relieve you from the stress you experience in your academic life?
   [multiple answers allowed]

a. carefully checking assignments' due dates and submitting them before the deadline.

b. having a chat with friends and teachers

c. having a nice lunch at the canteen.

d. joining a club or participating in volunteer activities

e. other (   )

Discuss and compare your answers with your classmates.

▶▶▶ Evaluate how much you know

You can explore the Internet or share your knowledge with your classmates about the information provided below.

1. Do you know about the United Nations' Sustainable Development Goals (SDGs)? How many goals do they have?

_____

_____

2. In Goal 3, 'Ensure healthy lives and promote well-being for all at all ages' is stated. However, achieving this aim is difficult. *Japan Health Policy Now* (2021) reports that in 2017, an estimated 4.19 million people in Japan were living with mental health issues, and this number is expected to continue to increase (para 1).* What do you think of this? Does your school provide counselling services to students?

> *インターネット上の記述を直接引用する場合、どのパラグラフに記述されていたのか、といった情報を(para 1)のように示します。この場合は、第1パラグラフ目にあったことを示しています。

_____

_____

▶▶▶ Writing

Read the following question, and write about 100 words.

Some people say that reading books is very important for shaping ideas and opinions. As there is not enough time to have all kinds of real-life experiences, reading allows one to experience a variety of things virtually. They also believe that time allotted* for reading books is good for maintaining their well-being because they can get away from the real world and organise their minds. Now, formulate an opinion that contrasts with this statement, taking the view 'reading books is not important for us'.   *allot （時間を）充てる

_____

_____

_____

▶▶ Vocabulary and expressions

Below is a list of words taken from Text. Match these with their synonyms in the right column.

1. drastically	a. view
2. maintain	b. keep
3. contribute to	c. aid
4. perspective	d. extremely
5. have a blast	e. have a great time

1. (   )   2. (   )   3. (   )   4. (   )   5. (   )

▶▶▶Text

🔊 Audio 05

Read a blog about lifestyle and answer the following questions.

News and Opinion > Lifestyle Blog> **Lifestyle** Changes due to the Worldwide COVID-19 Pandemic

Needless to say, the COVID-19 pandemic has **drastically** changed the way we live. Here are my suggestions for **maintaining** our well-being.

Written by Colin Wu, Student Support Office | 23 August 2021

Due to the worldwide COVID-19 pandemic, many people have been forced to stay home, and students can only attend classes online. Before the pandemic, we were free to have a chat with friends anytime and go outside without wearing a mask. The urban landscape has drastically changed due to the pandemic. This stresses me out. I'm often asked what an ideal healthy lifestyle is, but my life is rather unhealthy.

Having 'me time'

During the pandemic, I watched TV all day, stayed up late surfing the Internet, endlessly scrolled on social media, and watched YouTube videos. I clearly needed a lifestyle change. However, this begs the question: how can we maintain healthy lifestyles? By walking in the park or sticking to a healthy diet every day? These habits **contribute to** a healthy lifestyle. If I give them a try, then I could probably lose some weight... However, today, I suggest that you have a different **perspective**, that is, making time for 'me time'.

I love reading books, driving my car, and listening to jazz music. These activities make me happy. Even if I'm busy, I try to make time for them. I try to take time out of my schedule and devoting time just for me. During my free time (but, I 'create' me time), I often drive to my favourite café, and read a good novel there. **I have a blast!**

Some of you might have experienced cancelling an original schedule for another event or work. However, I rarely do this nowadays. I don't like to cancel my plans. I believe that creating 'me time' is very important to maintain one's mental health and well-being. However, you may soon realise that this is difficult in practice. For example, if you receive a message from a friend, you may be eager to respond immediately. Your smartphone may be to blame for this! How about turning off your phone for a while? Anyway, I recommend freeing up your schedule for your personal well-being. This is an important habit for a healthy university student.

Comments

5

▶▶▶ Comprehension questions

1. Who is the target audience of this blog?

   a. older people   b. students   c. parents   d. policymakers

2. What is the purpose of this article?

   a. To provide some tips for protection from COVID-19.
   b. To offer suggestions for maintaining one's physical health.
   c. To show how wonderful reading novels and listening to jazz music is.
   d. To give tips to improve one's well-being.

3. What does the author believe to be one of the best ways to stay in good mental health?

   a. freeing up his schedule
   b. keeping his schedule packed as much as possible
   c. writing a novel at a café while drinking a cup of coffee
   d. frequently having chats with his friends on his smartphone

▶▶▶ Discussions

To what extent do you agree with the following statements about maintaining good mental health? Insert check marks below. Remember that there are no right or wrong answers.

	5. Strongly agree	4. Agree	3. Neither agree nor disagree	2. Disagree	1. Strongly disagree
a. Singing your favourite song at the top of your lungs in a closed room.					
b. Eating at least one meal outside each day.					
c. Chilling out with friends at a café or restaurant.					
d. Getting plenty of sleep (i.e. more than 7 hours a day).					
e. Making an effort to maintain good relationships and chat with friends face-to-face.					
f. Frequently interacting with friends on social media.					

After answering these questions, list the things that help you stay mentally healthy and why (minimum of 50 words). Afterwards, share your opinions with your classmates.

_____

_____

_____

_____

_____

Pair or group work and critical thinking

With this textbook, you are encouraged to do pair or group work so that you can broaden your perspectives.*1 Each classmate has a different opinion and idea, thereby*2 enriching your learning because you can encounter different values and beliefs through language learning. Knowledge of different points of view can broaden our understanding, which is an essential component of critical thinking.

*1 perspective （物事に対する）視点　　*2 thereby それによって

2.2 | Browsing the Internet

People spend their time on smartphones while travelling in the Mass Rapid Transit train in Singapore.

Look at the photo and the caption. What came to your mind when you first saw this picture? Is the Singaporean lifestyle similar to yours?

▶▶▶Text

 Audio 06

Read a passage and answer the following questions.

Lifestyle advisor > staff blog>

Enrich Your Life

Many students **aspire** to spend less time on their smartphones, but they find it very difficult to do. How can you **reduce** the amount of time you spend on your phone?

Written by Kimiko YOSHIDA | 27 October 2023   5

How many hours a day do you spend browsing the Internet? About an hour for interacting with friends on social media? Or around two hours for watching video clips? Nowadays, it is difficult to imagine life without the Internet. According to the Japanese   10

Cabinet Office (2019), **approximately** 99% of senior high school students use the Internet, and about 66% of them access the Internet via their smartphones. The Cabinet Office also found that about 90% and 87% of them went online for communication purposes and to watch video clips, respectively.

15 Improving your social life

Most parents and teachers believe that **excessive** Internet use is **detrimental** for young adults. The Cabinet Office found that senior high school students in Japan spent an average of about four hours a day online, and most of this was just for recreation! Do you feel that this is short or long for senior high school students? I
20 personally think it is exceedingly long. Below is my idea of how you can reduce your Internet use:

▶ Be more sociable

Young adults also feel that spending excessive time online does not contribute to a productive lifestyle. Some of them use the term *ria-ju* (リア充-in Japanese) , which
25 means enjoying a real life or being sociable rather than just staying online. This term was first coined* in the early 2000s as Internet slang, and it has recently become popular among young adults who are trying to reduce their screen time. Get your eyes off the screen for a while and go outside.

▶ Make your own rules

30 Can you live without the Internet? I believe that using the Internet in moderation according to your personal needs is necessary for enriching your daily life. For instance, turning off your smartphone before going to bed.

▶ Switch up your routine

If checking your emails and social media is the first thing you do after getting up, then
35 try to complete other tasks such as taking a shower or drinking a glass of water first. These slight changes to your routine could reduce the time you spend online, as they are less difficult to do than to stay off the Internet.

*coin （新しい言葉を）作る

Comments

▶▶▶ Comprehension questions

1. What percentage of students went online for watching video clips?
   a. 66%   b. 87%   c. 90%   d. 99%

2. What is the main purpose of this article?
   a. To inform its readers that approximately two thirds of senior high school students are browsing the Internet.
   b. To demonstrate that Internet use is detrimental for young adults.
   c. To indicate suggestions on how to minimise screen time.
   d. To offer suggestions for using social media.

3. How does the register* type of the text appear?

    a. Ceremonial   b. Very formal   c. Semi-formal   d. Casual

*register: the level of formality in a piece of writing

Tips: Why is register important?

Being aware of register is an important skill in writing a text using an appropriate tone. If instructions for taking a medicine are too casual, things will feel unnatural. If a personal blogger introduces a nice type of cuisine in a local city, and the tone is exceedingly formal, you may feel that the author is unfriendly, and it may not attract readers. Therefore, it is important to adjust your register depending on writing scenarios.

▶▶▶ Vocabulary and expressions

Numbered 1-5 below is a list of words taken from Text. Match these words with their definitions from 'a' to 'e'.

1. aspire	a. too much
2. reduce	b. make less
3. approximately	c. nearly
4. excessive	d. harmful
5. detrimental	e. hope

1. (   )   2. (   )   3. (   )   4. (   )   5. (   )

▶▶▶ Discussions

1. The author mentions that 'Most parents and teachers believe that excessive Internet use is detrimental for young adults'. How much do you think this statement is true? Why?

_____

_____

_____

2. The author says, 'I personally think it is exceedingly long'. This statement seems subjective. Do you also think it is 'exceedingly long'? Why?

_____

_____

_____

3. Some students may feel that the author of the blog focuses on the fact that smartphone use is not good for maintaining one's well-being. Now, formulate an opposing opinion to that of the blogger with concise* reasons on 'Smartphone use can improve our well-being'. Write your opinion in between 80 to 120 words.

*concise 簡潔な

_____

_____

_____

_____

_____

_____

_____

_____

4. Compare your thoughts to those of your partner.

Answering critical-thinking level questions

Answering simple questions such as yes-no questions does not deepen your thinking. It only requires limited vocabulary and expressions, and you do not need to elaborate*[1] on your ideas and thoughts. Contrarily, answering critical-thinking level questions stimulates*[2] thinking and necessitates a wide variety of vocabulary and expressions. You must express your thoughts by using appropriate words and expressions. Therefore, such questions can improve English proficiency level.*[3]

*[1] elaborate ~を詳しく述べる   *[2] stimulate 刺激する   *[3] proficiency level 熟達度

▶▶▶ Writing

What is the purpose of posting a blog entry? Have you ever written this type of text before? Blogs often aim to provide their audience with advice, help, or useful information. They also include current topics with the author's original viewpoint. Below are tips on how to write a good blog entry.

---

a. Including a catchy heading

b. Indicating a date of entry

c. Starting with a compelling introduction

d. Imagining a target audience — the content should be simple and coherent

e. Mentioning a clear purpose for writing

f. Adopting a conversational style with a semi-formal to informal (personal) register

g. Supporting opinions with examples

Remember, as a blog entry may be read by numerous people worldwide, information should be evident, your opinions and thoughts are considerable—the content will be open to the public.

Question 1

Now, go back to Text and indicate which paragraphs are mostly aligned with 'a' to 'g'? What line(s) are these written on?

a. (   )   e. (   )
b. (   )   f. (   )
c. (   )   g. (   )
d. (   )

Question 2

Write a blog entry explaining the importance of maintaining our mental or physical health. When you write a blog entry, include all tips 'a' to 'g'. —(minimum of 200 words)

2.3 | Food loss and waste

▶▶▶ Guiding questions

1. How much food is lost or wasted in a year worldwide? Why is food loss or waste happening?

2. Some people say that food loss and waste result from our habits. To what extent is changing our habits difficult?

3. How can we act as young adults toward reducing food loss and waste? How might the world change?

Introduction

In this section, we would like to focus on 'lifestyle'. In our lifestyle, producing food and eating it is vital for maintaining our well-being. However, ample* food is lost or wasted worldwide, and this is becoming a significant issue for us. Some of us may think this issue is remote, but actually, this is a very close topic for us.

*ample: more than enough

▶▶▶ Warm-up

1. What did you eat for breakfast this morning? Did you eat everything?
2. If you found a hair in a dish at a restaurant, what would you do? Would you keep eating it or ask staff to replace the plate?

▶▶▶ Text

 Audio 07

The text below focuses on food loss and waste issues. Everyone knows food loss and waste happen worldwide, and ample food is produced in vain. Let us explore the facts of the issue and consider how we can act for reducing food loss and waste.

Read an article and answer the following questions.

How Can We Reduce Food Loss and Waste?

by Luna Cooper -1 February 2021

'*According to the UN report, more than 690 million people still perish as of 2015. To save hunger, UN declares* **Sustainable** *Development Goals* (SDGs), *and they are aiming to* 'end hunger, achieve **food security** *and improved nutrition and promote sustainable agriculture' by 2030* '.

5

10

About 14 percent of all food is lost and huge tons of food are wasted in a year around the world, according to the United Nations. This number is quite big! If the products do not meet the **aesthetic** standard, these may not be displayed in stores. Many companies have a strict standard, but due to this, many foods do not reach customers.

15

Differences Between 'Food Loss' and 'Food Waste'

We sometimes use the words 'food loss' and 'food waste' as a colocation2, but the meanings of these terms are slightly different. The term 'food loss' is used for 'before displaying food on shelves'. If a staff member finds an ugly shape or a scratched vegetable, these may not be displayed at a store. This means products are created to throw away! Food waste, in contrast, means 'after displaying on a shelf'. For instance, if 20 a product's sell-by day is overdue, it may not be sold for customers. Or, if a product goes bad in the fridge at your home, you should throw it away. Or, if you feel full, the food may be trashed. These things are called food waste.

Food Loss and Food Waste Burdens Our Planet

Why are food loss and food waste not good for us? When they create food, they need 25 many natural resources such as water and soil. In addition to this, they need to transport food from farms or factories to markets. During these processes, they produce much greenhouse gas. This **burden** our environment. Furthermore, losing food and wasting food hurts hungry people. There are large numbers of hungry people around the world. According to the UN report, more than 690 million people still perish as of 2015. 30

Actions for Reducing Food Waste

Not only understanding facts but also acting for reducing food loss and waste is important. I'd like to focus on what we can do for reducing food waste as a young adult. The ways below are not hard to try, they are simple, but these can contribute to creating a better planet.

35

1. Not buying too much food
   Buying an appropriate volume of food is important for reducing food waste. It also helps save you money.

2. Buying products which are displayed in the front of a shelf
40   Most supermarkets tend to display products in sell-by or best before order. Some of you may have witnessed or experienced getting products from the back, but from now on, let's buy products from the front.

3. Use a 'doggy bag'
   If a meal is too much for you, do not leave food on the plate, but ask a staff member
45   let you take home. Some restaurants may prepare a doggy bag for you.

4. Understand Expiration Dates
   In the UK, labels 'best before'(taste good terms), 'sell by' (displaying terms), and 'use by' have been commonly used. Recently, some supermarkets only use 'use by' for reducing tons of food waste.

50   You can do these four things from today. You don't have to think the issue difficult!

Updated 3 November 2023

Go back to TOP

▶▶▶ Vocabulary and expressions

In Text, four words were in BOLD. Choose the definitions from the right-hand column that matches the meaning of the highlighted words from the text on the left.

1. sustainable	**a.** that causes worry, difficulty or hard work
2. food security	**b.** that can continue or be continued for a long time
3. aesthetic	**c.** the state of having reliable access to enough healthy food that you can afford
4. burden	**d.** connected with beauty

1. (   )   **2.** (   )   **3.** (   )   **4.** (   )

▶▶▶ Comprehension questions

1. Who is the target audience?

2. What is the main purpose of this article?

3. According to the United Nations, how much food is lost worldwide annually?

4. What are the differences between 'food loss' and 'food waste'?

5. Why are food loss and waste detrimental*?

*detrimental: causing harm or damage

▶▶▶ Discussions

1. Have you ever been involved with food waste before? Can you share your experience with your classmates?

2. To what extent do you believe the actions suggested by the author are effective for reducing food waste? If everyone tries these actions, how much can food waste be resolved?

▶▶▶ Writing

Create your three original ways for reducing food loss and waste. After that, propose them to your classmates.

1) _____

2) _____

3) _____

2.4 | Writing a better content for a blog

▶▶▶ Text

🔊 Audio 08

Read the passage and answer the following questions.

The Internet is widely used globally in a modern society. The majority of people use the Internet for searching for
5 information. However, some of them may use it for providing information. For instance, you have posted a picture or a comment on Instagram, or you
10 have tweeted something on

Twitter. These social media are easy to post and your content can be read by many people. Soon, you may be required to post content not only on social media, but also for web articles. In this session, we would like to explore the effective skills for how to write a better blog.

15 What are the effective ways to write a fascinating article in English? Below are six simple ways to get the attention from your readers.

1. Know your audience
Think about the target audience. Who would read your article? Internet users are varied, so you should decide the target audience. You are not
20 recommended to imagine 'unspecified', but set a specific audience at first.

2. Create a 'catchy' title

Readers will decide whether an article contains necessary information in seconds. A title should be concise and contains what you mostly would like to say. If necessary, you can add an important quotation, which is written in an article at the top.
25

3. Write simple sentences and avoid jargon* as much as you can

Readability is important for an article. Even though you know a lot about a topic, the level of knowledge about the topic is different for your audience. Make sure information is understandable for every target audience.

4. Use active voice
30

For a website article, active voice is preferable rather than passive voice. This is because, audience can feel your article to be friendly when you use active voice. For instance, instead of writing 'A beautiful flower can be found in the picture', write 'You can find a beautiful flower in the picture'.

5. Provide precise information
35

Consider that information in your article is correct and your references are appropriate. Your contents will be read by many people, and they may believe everything you wrote. Get your classmates to read it for you. This will give you multi-dimensional perspectives on your article.

6. Interact with your audience
40

Keep audience interest with your article through doing 'interaction' with them. For having 'interaction' with them, asking your audience some questions (with their answers) could be a good way of involving them.

*jargon 専門語

▶▶▶ True or False

Write '**T**' if the sentence is true, and '**F**' if the sentence is false.

1. Instagram and Twitter are categorised as social media. (   )
2. Considering the target audience is not so important. (   )
3. Creating a catchy title is more important than writing simple sentences. (   )
4. Using jargon is important to show your talent. (   )
5. Providing ample information without considering its accuracy is not recommended. (   )
6. Asking a tricky question is acceptable to attract an audience's interest. (   )

▶▶▶ Writing

Write a blog entry (minimum of 200 words) for university students, introducing a nice spot for refreshing your mind. Please note that the tone of the blog is friendly, and readers may feel eager to visit this location. Additionally, when you write it, refer to the suggestions listed in the Text on pages 50-51 and the tips listed below.

a. Including a catchy heading
b. Indicating a date of entry
c. Starting with a compelling introduction
d. Imagining a target audience
e. Mentioning a clear purpose for writing
f. Adopting a conversational style with a semi-formal to informal (personal) register
g. Supporting opinions with examples

▶▶▶ Grammar for writing

**Wordiness (the use of many words to deliver an idea)
should be avoided in your writing!**

The use of many words to deliver your idea can complicate the message and divert the target reader's attention. Therefore, in writing, ideas need to be delivered as concisely as possible.
e.g. 'all over the world' → 'globally' or 'worldwide'.

Avoiding wordiness can also lend a more formal tone to the sentence.
e.g. little by little → gradually

Further examples:
Avoid: As a result, school in Japan has gradually grown since…
Better: Consequently, school in Japan has gradually grown since….
Avoid: The idea has been studied by a number of researchers…
Better: The idea has been studied by several researchers…
Avoid: However, debates and discussions regarding the use of the Internet have not yet been terminated.
Better: However, debates and discussions regarding the use of the Internet continue today.

**Redundancy: the unnecessary repetition of words or ideas. It should be
avoided in writing!**

In your writing, ideas need to be delivered as concisely as possible and the use of expressions should be concise.

e.g.

Redundant: The girl was bored throughout the entire play.

*the word 'throughout' means during the whole time or period and already implies 'entire'.

Suggested revision: The girl was bored throughout the play.

Redundant : I love reading a book. I love driving a car. I love listening to Jazz music.

Suggested revision: I love reading books, driving my car, and listening to jazz music.

▶▶▶ Reflection

1. How have your thoughts about well-being changed? What was your take-away information about the concept of well-being?

_____

_____

2. How much did you understand the tips for writing a blog and a web article? Do you think you adhered* to the tips indicated in this part? If you were to mark your blog entry between 1 to 6 (one is poor and six is best), what would your score be and why?

*adhere: to stick firmly

_____

_____

3. Compare your answers with those of your partner.

Why do we need critical thinking in English learning?

Vygotsky, a well-known linguist, asserts[1] that thinking about something and learning a language are inextricably[2] linked. For example, before you say anything, you should all think about it. Critical thinking, in particular, necessitates a wide range of words and expressions, rather than simply considering a single question. Additionally, some studies have explained the relationship between critical thinking and English proficiency levels. These reports clarify that if language learners' level of critical thinking is high, their English proficiency level is also high.

[1] assert: to state clearly and definitely that something is true
[2] inextricably 切っても切れないほどに

Part 3

Technology and Interaction

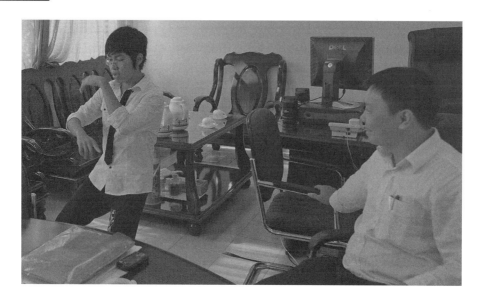

1. Look at the photo. What are they doing?
2. Read the statement below. How much do you agree with this? Why?
   'Performing dance is a very useful tip for overcoming game addiction. Hence, the government should promote a cyber addict treatment programme by making them perform dancing'.

   agree / partially agree / partially disagree / disagree

   Why? _____

   _____

3. Below are two people's responses to the statement above. Which opinion do you support? Why?

   A: Some young adults play online games a lot. I believe it is not good for them in terms of maintaining their mental health. Some studies show that if they play them a lot, players tend to be aggressive to others. So, they should consider reducing the amount of time they spend playing it.

   B: Many young adults love to play online games. I strongly believe gaming enriches our life. Recently, some games are recognised as sports, and their status has been gradually improving. People should understand good effects of playing online games.

   Which opinion? _____

   Why? _____

   _____

   _____

The aims of this part:

1) Explore how social media and email have changed the ways people interact with each other.
2) Reflect on your relationships with social media and technology as well as their respective roles.
3) Explore the essential components of writing a formal email and compose it with an appropriate tone.

Introduction

The Internet is our 'lifeline'. You may often search the Internet to find some information. Some of you may have experienced reading a professional article on a website, and using the information for their references in an academic talk. Reading an article on the web is a vital skill in your academic life.

3.1 | Fake news

▶▶▶ Guiding questions

1. When you check social media or news, do you frequently consider whether the information is reliable? Which information resources do you consider to be trustworthy? Why do you think so?

   Which information resources? _____

   Why? _____

   _____

2. When do we use email? List at least three reasons why we use email.

   1) _____

   2) _____

   3) _____

3. Let us reflect on your relationships with social media and internet technology. How has technology changed the ways in which people interact?

   _____

   _____

▶▶▶ Evaluate how much you know

1. How do you obtain the most recent information? Do you acquire it from Instagram, Twitter, online news, television, newspapers, or other sources?

_____

_____

_____

2. The Internet is the primary source of information for most students, and you are at risk of exposure to fake news. You may also inadvertently*¹ share the fake news without first verifying its veracity.*² Have you ever encountered fake news? How much trust do you place in online news sites?   *¹ inadvertently うっかり、何の気なしに   *² veracity 信ぴょう性

_____

_____

_____

_____

▶▶▶ Vocabulary and expressions

The following words will appear in Text. Before reading the text, look up the meaning of any words that you do not know well.

a. fact-checking	**e.** trustworthy
b. resource	**f.** reliable
c. attachment	**g.** ideology
d. accurate	**h.** subjective

▶▶▶ Text Audio 09

Read an email and answer the following questions.

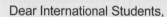

Subject:	Developing your fact-checking skills	

Dear International Students,

We are extremely pleased to see many students back on our campuses. Our Australian campuses are moving towards 'the new COVID-19 normal' conditions.

Last year's most used buzz term was 'fake news'. We often encounter it online, and it sometimes negatively affects your academic life. Strathfield University strongly encourages international students to develop fact-checking skills to reach appropriate resources.

Attached is the information released by the Media System Centre. Please find the file and check its contents.

Let us know if you have any questions.

Best regards,
Martin Nguyen

Attached

Strathfield University Media System Centre
David Smith

Why should we care about fake news?

The ability to discern*1 accurate information is an essential skill you will use in your academic life. More Strathfield University students than ever are receiving abundant*2 news from social media, but this news tend to elicit*3 a strong emotional impact in readers. Before and while reading an article on the topic, let us ask you four questions below. These will help you ascertain*4 whether an article is trustworthy.

1. Who produced the article?
Is the author reliable? Knowing information about the author is important. If the author is sponsored by a company or a political party, you should be critical regarding whether his/her opinions may be ideological or biased.

2. Is the evidence provided in an article reliable?
How did the author discover the information? Does the author merely describe an opinion based on his/her subjective viewpoints or use evidence? You need to carefully check whether the evidence is sufficient.

3. Is there any missing information?
Some posts on social media tend to overlook inconvenient truths. Some authors want to only introduce positive information. Critically consider whether the negative information is overlooked.

4. Are the photos authentic?
In the past and currently, numerous authors have tended to broadcast fake news using a doctored*5 photo. Check whether the photo depicts the truth.

Please do not share an article on social media if you are unsure of its veracity. More accuracy checklists are available here: https://strathfieldfield-university.edu/mediacentre/fakenews

*1 discern 見分ける   *2 abundant （有り余るほどの）多くの   *3 elicit （感情や反応などを）引き起こす
*4 ascertain = to find out the true or correct information about something
*5 doctor (something) = to change something in order to trick somebody

▶▶▶ Comprehension questions

1. What is the main purpose of the email?

    a. To provide information to international students to protect them from fake news.

    b. To inform readers that fake news always defrauds* international students.

    c. To announce that David Smith is in charge of the Media System Centre.

    d. To discourage international students from using unauthorised social networks.

*defraud だます

2. What is NOT mentioned in the text?

    a. The faculty hopes to improve the fact-checking skills of international students.

    b. Because it is difficult to determine whether the news is reliable or not, international students should avoid using social media.

    c. It is important to assess whether the article overlooked negative information or not.

    d. Some fake news is also broadcast with a fabricated photo.

3. What action would readers take after reading the attachment?

    a. To share the attached document with their friends

    b. Reply to Martin Nguyen to inform him that the email was received safely.

    c. To be careful not to share untrustworthy content and check the hyperlinked information.

    d. To contact Mr. David Smith if they have further queries.

▶▶▶ Discussions

Answer the questions below.

1. In the Text, the author mentions that if the author is sponsored by a company or a political party, you should be critical regarding whether his/her opinions may be ideological or biased. However, is the information provided by the local government reliable? To what extent do you think that all the information provided by them is reliable?

_____

_____

_____

_____

2. Around the world, we can find a variety of sources to get information. Which of the following resources reliable? Rate each source from 1 (Not reliable at all) to 5 (Highly reliable).

a. Wikipedia		f. TV news	
b. Paper dictionary		g. YouTuber's comment	
c. A reviewed academic paper		h. A post on Twitter	
d. A blog		i. Online news resources	
e. A government report			

After rating, give reasons and examples why you rate them so, and share your thoughts with your partner.

_____

_____

_____

_____

Information & technology, and critical thinking

In everyday life, you are bombarded[*1] with information from the Internet, TV, advertisements, and newspapers. You will find that the quality of the information varies. Some of it may be fake, or some may be too subjective[*2] and lack evidence. Identifying the most relevant information key to making an appropriate judgement.

Regarding improving English reading proficiency, most English texts are written with the authors' arguments (claims and reasons) and facts. Facts are often displayed after an argument to strengthen the author's stance. As a result, by focusing on what an argument and facts are, one can understand the article's main point. This process can improve one's ability to quickly grasp the necessary information.

[*1] bombard: here, the word is used as 'received too much information'   [*2] subjective 主観的

3.2 | Formal email

▶▶▶ Evaluate how much you know

1. Have you ever sent formal emails to someone? What are the essential elements of a formal email? List three essential components of a formal email below.

- _____
- _____
- _____

2. Is it polite to communicate via social media or email in your group (a research group, workplace, or club activity), if you have an important message, such as your absence from an event and an arrival delay?

_____
_____

▶▶▶ Text

 Audio 10

Three students of Bundai University are joining in a collaborative research project with members of Northern University in Singapore. They are now preparing an oral session for an academic conference, and they have created a questionnaire for a survey.

To:	Sarah Chan, Lim Tan, Kim Zhang
Cc:	Ami Nakajima, Tomoki Takeuchi
From:	Yurika Sato
Sent:	February 4, 3:35 p.m.
Subject:	Regarding the pre-survey results
Attached:	poster_conference

Dear Sarah, Lim, and Kim,
(Cc Ami, and Tomoki).

I hope this email finds you well. I have emailed you to share what the members from Bundai University are doing for our research. As discussed in the last Zoom session on January 17, the Bundai members distributed a pre-survey draft questionnaire to 62 participants last week, and we have collected their answers and analysed the data. The results of the questionnaire are attached herewith.

By conducting a pre-survey, we have arrived at the following suggestions for the questionnaire:

- Some participants were unable to understand the meanings of some questions, so we should revise the questions' words and expressions.
- Many participants spent more than 20 minutes answering questions. Therefore, we should shorten the questionnaire to reduce the burden on the participants.

In summary, I think it is better to upgrade the questionnaire in terms of expressions and reduce the volume.

The due date for the submission of the abstract for the conference is March 30. How about we moderate the questionnaire and distribute it to targeted participants by the end of February? To accomplish this, we also reviewed the results of the pre-survey, and I look forward to hearing from you at the start of next week.

Best,
Yurika

To:	Yurika Sato, Ami Nakajima, Tomoki Takeuchi
Cc:	Lim Tan, Kim Zhang
From:	Sarah Chan
Sent:	February 4, 8:35 p.m.
Subject:	Re: Regarding the pre-survey results

Dear Yurika, Ami and Tomoki,
CC Lim, and Kim,

Thank you very much for your comment. Our Northern University members conducted a pre-survey two days prior, and we found similar problems as your team pointed out. We also believe that the questionnaire should be added for the purpose of this study and research ethics.

We have a big assignment due this week, and we need to submit it by the end of February, so if possible (we know this is a bit tight on the schedule), could you move the due date to the first week of March?

Thank you for your consideration.

Best,
Sarah

▶▶▶ Comprehension questions

1. What is the main purpose of these emails?
   a. To ask for analysis of the survey
   b. To share the collaborated research progress
   c. To tell that the number of participants is too small
   d. To suggest the postponement of the due date of submission of the poster

2. What does Yurika NOT want to do for senders?
   a. She wants to decide the date for moderating the questionnaire.
   b. She asked senders to check the result of the pre-survey.
   c. She wants to receive their feedback by the end of February.
   d. She want to receive their email by tomorrow.

3. What problems were found in the pre-survey? Choose two answers.
   a. All questions are not appropriate for the survey.
   b. The length of the questionnaire is slightly long for the participants.
   c. Some questions are difficult to understand.
   d. The number of participants should be more than 62.

4. Most formal emails contain the following elements in their texts:

---

a. Personal greeting

At the beginning of the email, put receivers' name(s) with a title (if necessary) (Dear Mr../ Ms. , to whom it may concern). No names or beginning with 'Hi' would be informal.
Dear Dr. …or Ms. or Mr. …, Dear First Name (if readers are also students or a colleague), To whom it may concern (if you do not know a specific reader)

b. Direct opening

The first paragraph could be a direct opening: state the purpose(s) why you are writing an email. Readers may receive many messages in a day or are busy, so you should briefly explain the purpose.

c. Concise argument

The second paragraph could be a concise argument that explains the details. You should try to shorten the paragraph so that readers can understand your arguments.

d. Clear call to action

The last paragraph should be a call to action; you should mention what readers should do after reading an email.

e. Formal sign off

Conclude your email with a salutation such as 'Kind regards,' or 'Best,' (less formal). Then put your signature after it. In a formal email, a full name is required, but signing your first name is acceptable in a less formal situation.

Now, indicate the features in email and put -a- to -e- in the text below.

Dear Sarah, Lim, and Kim, 【   】
(Cc Ami, and Tomoki).

I hope this email finds you well. I have emailed you to share what the members from Bundai University are doing for our research. 【   】 As discussed in the last Zoom session on January 17, the Bundai members distributed a re-survey draft questionnaire to 62 participants last week, and we have collected their answers and analysed the data. The results of the questionnaire are attached herewith.

By conducting a pre-survey, we have arrived at the following suggestions for the questionnaire:
- Some participants were unable to understand the meanings of some questions, so we should to revise the questions' words and expressions.
- Many participants spent more than 20 minutes answering questions. Therefore, we should shorten the questionnaire to reduce the burden on the participants.

In summary, I think it is better to upgrade the questionnaire in terms of expressions and reduce the volume. 【   】

The due date for the submission of the abstract for the conference is March 30. How about we moderate the questionnaire and distribute it to targeted participants by the end of February? To accomplish this, we also reviewed the results of the pre-survey, and I look forward to hearing from you at the start of next week. 【   】

Best,
Yurika 【   】

▶▶▶ Discussions

1. The Bundai students and students of Northern University have been exchanging their research progress via email. Do you believe that this style of interaction is the best approach in this situation? Or do you have any better suggestions for their interaction? Give specific reasons for your opinion.

_____

_____

_____

_____

2. In Text, Sarah responded to the message in six hours. Some people may believe it is better to respond as soon as possible, ideally within 24 hours. Do we need to respond to the message soon? Do you really think we should react soon?

_____

_____

_____

_____

3. Email is a very convenient tool for individuals to communicate with one another. Even when they live apart and are spread around the world, the message is conveyed quickly. However, others claim that there are certain disadvantages to communicating via email. Can you guess the reason for these claims? List the possible reasons for this.

_____

_____

_____

_____

4. Share your thoughts with your partner. How are your partners' thoughts similar to or different from those of yours?

3.3 | How to write a formal email

▶▶ Warm-up

Examine the image. A person is checking an email on a computer screen. According to AFP, over 55 percent of employed Americans checked their emails over the holidays in 2010. How about you? Do you frequently check your email or the messages on your apps? Many people receive messages from their schools, teachers, or workplaces during the holidays. How do you feel about that?

Now, share your thoughts with your partner.

▶▶ Text

 Audio 11

Finding part-time jobs while at university is an important task for most students. In English-speaking countries, most institutions and companies require students to send 'a cover letter'. A cover letter is a document you send with your resume (CV). Nowadays, they accept it via email, and its style is mostly the same as explained in section 3.2. Read an email and answer the following questions.

| Date: | December 3, 2023 4:32 pm |
| Subject: | Regarding staff recruiting |

To whom it may concern,

I am Yuki Imagawa, a fourth-year student at the School of Commerce. Please accept my application for a part-time math teaching assistant position in a state middle school. I believe you will find my academic qualifications acceptable for your position.

I have volunteered as a middle school math student teacher at a local school for two years. I am confident about my expertise in statistics, and subject knowledge of math. I am currently part of a teacher training course and have a 3.7 GPA. In the future, I would like to be a full-time math teacher in a middle school, and I believe that I have enough skill to become one.

I am certain that my knowledge and the experiences I have gained at middle school as a student teacher will be highly valuable in this position.

I look forward to meeting you soon. Thank you very much for your time and consideration. If you have any questions, please let me know.

Sincerely,
Yuki Imagawa
Imagawa.yuki@u-londonbridge.ac.uk

▶▶▶ Comprehension questions

If the sentences below are correct, put 'T' for True, and if incorrect, put 'F' for False. Justify your answers only for the ones which are false (no need to justify if true).

1. The main purpose of this email is to apply for a full-time math teacher position. (   )

    Justification: _____

2. Yuki has been a part-time math teacher in middle school. (   )

    Justification: _____

3. Yuki requested the readers to reply to her message as soon as possible. (   )

    Justification: _____

▶▶▶ Discussions

Answer the questions below.

1. Do you prefer to use social media or email to contact your friends, members of your club, and teachers? Can you explain the advantages and disadvantages of its use?

    _____

    _____

    _____

2. In modern society, many people rely on technology. Much of information related to academics is delivered by Learning Management System (LMS) or email, and your lecturer may contact you via email. In contrast, some people do not like to use email because they claim that even during their holidays, the app alerts them about receiving emails. Now, formulate an opinion around this statement: 'We do not need emails at all in our university life'.

    _____

    _____

    _____

    _____

    _____

3. The email below is to inform your teacher that you will be absent from next week's class due to a job interview. Find three major incorrect sentences that do not meet the formal email standard, and revise these sentences. After that, compare your answer with your partner's, and explain why you chose these sentences.

Date:	October 9, 2023 5:21 pm
Subject :	from Yuki (student number: B1W00043)

Hi Harris,

Hello. I am Yuki a fourth-year student at the School of Commerce. I will be absent the lesson next week due to the job interview attendance. Please accept my apologies for the delay in informing you know about my absence.

If I need to submit any assignments, would you let me know?
Thank you for your consideration.

Cheers,
Yuki

1. _____

   Revision: _____

2. _____

   Revision: _____

3. _____

   Revision: _____

▶▶▶ Writing

Imagine you are a first-year student at a Japanese university, and you have been selected to spend a year in Australia. You received the following email from a member of the staff at the International Liaison Office of the Australian Strathfield University.

Question: Read the following email and reply to this message.
Note: When you write an email, keep your tone formal, and refer to the elements mentioned in Section 3.2.

From:	Michael Griffiss
Sent:	Wednesday, 10 July 2023 1:45 PM
To:	Natsuki Ito
Subject:	Visiting Australia

Hi Natsuki,

I hope you are doing well and are looking forward to visiting Australia next semester. Could you please let me know the following details so that I can plan your courses?

1. Please let me know your current English proficiency level (test score) because all international students who do not meet the criteria must take our EAP (English for Academic Purposes) Course for a couple of months before enrolling for courses.
2. Your main campus is in New South Wales, however, one of the courses you plan to enrol for (EILE1193: Advanced Information Technology) will be held at the Queensland Campus. It seems that your registration was incorrect, therefore, may I change your course to a similar one (EILE1243: Media Literacy) that will be held at the New South Wales campus?
3. Our office is now arranging your accommodations. Could you let me know your preference: doing a homestay, a share accommodation, or at a boarding house? Do you have any special requests?

If you have any questions, please let me know!

Kind regards,
Michael Griffiss
International Liaison Officer | Australian Strathfield University
1191 Strathfield Road, Virginia, NSW 5019
E:michael.grifiss@asu.edu.au

▶▶▶ Grammar for writing

The use of 'which' and 'that'

The pronouns 'which' and 'that' —'which' is used to introduce nonessential information, while 'that' is used to include essential information.

Avoid: A teacher should use a speech rubric <u>which</u> aims to evaluate students' skills and knowledge.

Better: A teacher should use a speech rubric <u>that</u> aims to evaluate students' skills and knowledge.

The sentence above implies that the rubric is incidentally aimed to evaluate students, while the sentence below implies that the rubric is very essential to evaluate students' skills and knowledge.

▶▶▶ Reflection

1. What has most influenced your thoughts about the manner in which people interact as a result of internet technology?

_____

_____

2. What and how can you incorporate what you have learned in this section into your academic life or personal life?

_____

_____

3. Share your thoughts with your classmates. Are your classmates' ideas similar to or different from yours?

Part 4

Consistency and Rationale

1. Look at the photo. What came to your mind when you first saw this picture?

2. The caption under the photo reads: What changed your first impression?

> Matilde (R) and Marlene Pimentel, sisters, and university students attended a virtual class from a treetop on a hill, where they received an internet signal, in El Salvador, on August 21, 2020.

The aims of this part:

1. To explore the concepts of consistency and rationale and how these concepts affect our principles and thoughts.
2. To learn the features of an argumentative essay.
3. To develop the skills to write an effective argumentative essay with critical thinking.

4.1 | Reading an argumentative essay

Introduction
Throughout your academic life, you will learn the features and elements of an argumentative essay. You will write a large number of essays to express your thoughts. You will also present your argument in a concise and coherent manner to readers to encourage them to understand your thoughts.

In this part, you will explore the essence of an argumentative essay with critical thinking features, and write an essay aligned with these characteristics. After writing the essay, you will receive your friends' feedback. Peer reading and editing are essential activities to develop your writing skills, and some studies reveal that peer-reviewing has an effect similar to receiving feedback from teachers.

▶▶▶ Text
🔊 Audio 12

Read the passage and answer the following questions.

Before the COVID-19 pandemic, most universities offered classes face-to-face, and most students believed that it was normal. Of
5 course, some universities have already offered classes online as a form of distant learning. The pandemic, however, had a great impact on changing
10 students' learning styles. Many universities worldwide began to offer classes online, and students were forced not to come to university, and they needed to join the courses through an on-demand or real-time style. Many people point out that
15 offering classes online has its advantages and disadvantages. Therefore, some students love to attend classes online, while others do not.

A student wrote an essay (between 350-400 words) giving her opinion about the passage.

Due to the spread of COVID-19, university students' learning styles have drastically changed. Some universities locked out students and faculty from campus. However, thanks to the technology, students can attend online classes. Soon, many of them found that even though an online course guaranteed their right to learn, the satisfaction of learning was very different from face-to-face classes. 【　　】Of course, I understand some merits of online classes, but I do think face-to-face is better than online for the following reasons. 【　　】

First, we can easily interact face-to-face with other classmates. I found an article in which some experts in education advocate that we can deepen our knowledge and skills through interaction among students. 【　　】I also agree with this statement because in my personal experience, I can broaden my perspectives by knowing others' ideas and thinking. Some people may argue that an online course can also offer an opportunity for interaction among students 【　　】; however, I believe that its quality is slightly different. Via online learning, we tend to become more serious, but face-to-face, we can relax and become eager to chat with classmates with less hesitation. 【　　】

Second, we can deepen our understanding of human relationships between students and teachers. I believe that the purpose of learning at university is not only to gain subject knowledge and skills but also to learn how to build a good human relationship with others. In a book that I read yesterday; a sociologist points out that the most important role of school is to offer opportunities to build relationships for survival as a human race. My mother was the chief of the student's research group when she was at university. She often told me about this and believed that her experiences strengthened her leadership skills. 【　　】Some may think that we can also learn how to build a human relationship online because we can chat via the screen. 【　　】However, I completely disagree because it is difficult to read minds online. 【　　】

In summary, the face-to-face learning style is more effective than online in terms of broadening our perspectives by interacting with each other and learning how to build good human relationships. Some students love classes online, but I strongly recommend that they attend classes face-to-face. 【　　】

▶▶▶ Comprehension questions

1. What does the student write in the introduction?
   a. The student complains about the university offering courses online.
   b. The student mentions the social background of the topic and writes a thesis statement.
   c. The student states the pros and cons of online courses.

2. What are the student's arguments? Choose all answers.
   a. The student believes that they tend to become more serious via online courses.
   b. The student believes they can deepen human relationships through face to face learning.
   c. The student argues that an online course may not offer an opportunity for interaction.
   d. The student claims that an online learning style is more effective than face to face.

3. What are the characteristics of this essay? Choose all answers.
   a. The essay reinforces the student's subjective perspectives.
   b. The essay consists of an introduction, body, and conclusion.
   c. The tone of the essay is casual.
   d. The essay includes some pieces of evidence.
   e. The essay restates the authors' thesis statement and summarises all the arguments mentioned in the body paragraphs at the end of this essay.

▶▶▶ Key features of an argumentative essay

The structure of an argumentative essay should be straightforward so that readers can easily understand the author's logical consequences. The tone of the essay should not be too casual but should maintain a semi-formal or formal tone. The purpose of the essay is to take a stance on some issues. However, the use of vocabulary and expressions should be considered to avoid using difficult jargon because target readers may not have expertise relating to the topic. The following elements are the essential features of an argumentative essay:

1. Introductory paragraph and thesis statement
   The first paragraph of your argumentative essay should **refer to the general information or provide the background of the topic**. The introductory paragraph should also **include the thesis statement**. It is your main claim and should be presented concisely in one sentence.

2. Body paragraphs
   In the second paragraph, you should **explain the reasons for supporting your thesis statement** mentioned at the end of the introductory paragraph. A typical argumentative essay comprises two, three, or more body paragraphs **with some pieces of evidence**. In addition, to maintain multidimensional viewpoints, your essay should **introduce the recognition of opposition** (see page 77). Finally, to align with your thesis statement and to **refute the opposite view** (see page 77), you should mention regulations to be more persuasive to your readers.

3. Conclusion

In the conclusion section, you may **summarise supporting paragraphs and your primary argument by paraphrasing the thesis statement**. You do not normally introduce new information. This part should comprise at least two or three sentences because a paragraph does not consist of only one sentence.

Question: Now, go back to Text and write the features displayed 'a' to 'g' to the blank
【　　】.

    a. refer to general information or provide background of the topic

    b. include the thesis statement

    c. explain the reasons for supporting your thesis statement

    d. display some pieces of evidence

    e. introduce recognition of opposition

    f. refute the opposite view

    g. summarise supporting paragraphs and your primary argument by paraphrasing the thesis statement

▶▶▶ Discussions

1. In Text, the student emphasizes the merits of face-to-face classes, but as you know, an online class also has some merits. Can you provide a counterargument to the student? (Writing approximately 50 words).

_____

_____

_____

_____

_____

2. Share your thoughts with your partner.

4.2 | Evaluating an argumentative essay

A police officer is looking for evidence outside.

1. Look at the photo and caption. Pieces of evidence may be important clues for solving a case; therefore, it is very important to use evidence. In turn, evidence could also be important in academic context. Why do you think this is important in this context?

_____

_____

2. The term 'evidence' refers to a wide range of things. Can you list some evidence in an academic context? List a minimum of three items.

1) _____

2) _____

3) _____

3. Share your thoughts with your partner.

Read the passage and answer the following questions.

We will explore the essence of an argumentative essay. In this section, let us explore specific features of it more.

As explained earlier, in the introductory paragraph, we must include a thesis statement (= what you mostly want to claim in the essay), but it needs to
5 be supported by reason(s). Normally, the reasons are provided in the body paragraphs. If you do not provide a reason, it is not a 'claim,' but rather your 'opinion.'

In the body of the essay, you may support the thesis statement with evidence. Evidence comes in many forms, including personal experiences, research
10 studies, statistics, citing authorities, facts, and logical explanations. The body of the essay may also include recognition of opposition and refutations. These elements can strengthen your argument because they can show that you have already critically analysed the topic.

An important aspect of writing an argumentative essay is not to include
15 fallacies. Fallacies are reasoning errors. They occur when reason does not adequately support the claim in one of many ways. Therefore, during and after your writing, you must carefully consider whether your paragraphs are aligned with logical sequences.

Now, look at the chart on the next page that shows the elements of an
20 argumentative essay with critical thinking features.

Elements of an augmentative essay

Elements	Details
1. Arguments	Each argument consists of a claim supported by a reason. Claims are often expressed using claim markers such as 'I think' or 'In my opinion'. Reasons are statements used to support claims and generally answer why the claim should be believed.
2. Pieces of Evidence	Evidence constitutes statements or assertions[*1] which serve to strengthen the argument. Evidence comes in many forms including personal experience, research studies, statistics, citing authorities, facts and logical explanations.
3. Recognition of opposition	Opposing viewpoints constitute[*2] statements that run counter or offer alternative interpretations[*3] to those expressed in the claim.
4. Refutations	Refutations are statements in which the writer responds to the opposing viewpoint in a way that shows that it is inadequate[*4] in some way. Opposing viewpoints and refutations are identified by indicator phrases and words such as,'It is said that … but,', 'Some people claim that … however,'. Conjunctive devices, including 'although', 'despite', and 'even though'.
5. ✗ Fallacies (should be avoided)	Fallacies are errors in reasoning. They occur when the reason does not adequately[*5] support the claim in one of many ways.

(Adapted from Stapleton, 2001, pp. 536–539)

[*1] assertions = a statement saying that you strongly believe something to be true
[*2] constitute 〜の構成要素となる   [*3] interpretations 解釈   [*4] inadequate 不十分な   [*5] adequately 十分に

The chart shows the elements of argumentative essays with critical thinking. Some studies have clarified that when you include elements 1-4, your critical thinking and English writing skills may improve. Particularly, including the recognition of opposition (element 3) and refutations (element 4) are important in terms of broadening your perspectives.

▶▶▶ Comprehension questions

If the sentences below are correct, put '**T**' for True, and if incorrect, put '**F**' for False. Justify your answers only for the ones which are false (no need to justify if true).

1. An opinion is a set of claims and reasons. (   )

   Justification: _____

2. The writer of an argumentative essay should include pieces of evidence to support their thesis statement. (   )

   Justification: _____

3. The types of evidence vary, but personal experiences should not be used as evidence. (   )

   Justification: _____

4. The recognition of opposition and refutation is an important feature for writing the introductory paragraph. (　　)

Justification: _____

5. A paragraph containing fallacies is a good feature of an argumentative essay. (　　)

Justification: _____

Tips for critical thinking — Facts and claims

Identifying an author's opinion or an argument in the text is an important skill in learning critical thinking and improving your English reading skills. In terms of critical thinking, an author aims to tell his/her statements to listeners/readers through a text, and most of them include his personal opinion or an argument. But an opinion and an argument are different: opinion is the authors' subjective viewpoint without reasons, but an argument is a set of a claim that is supported by reasons. When we determine whether the authors' claims are verifiable* or not, we must check for certainty of reasons, and this is an important element of critical thinking.

*verifiable 検証できる

▶▶▶ Evaluating an argumentative essay

Here is a question and a sample of a student's response.

In an urban area, one can find a variety of restaurants, and some students enjoy having their lunch there. In contrast, others prefer to stay on campus and enjoy their lunchboxes. Which do you prefer?

✘ Poor essay example

I prefer to eat out rather than having a lunchbox. I rarely bring a lunchbox to university. If my friends cook theirs, I think it's really great but I just can't do that. There are several reasons for this. First, I am a long sleeper and it's really difficult to wake up in the mornings. I am really not good at waking up. Even if I have classes in the 1st period, I sometime wake up at the exact time the class starts! If I cook my lunch, I will be even more delayed getting to class. Some people may say that I ought to get up early, but it is very difficult to wake up! Second, I really enjoy hot meals and they help me to feel motivated to study. I know I could use a microwave to heat food in a lunchbox because students use it at the canteen for free. However, I often have a huge number of reports to complete. To tackle these, I need to know I can have a hot meal in a restaurant. My father also loves to eat out, so I believe the way I feel may be inherited from my father. Third, actually this is not just for me it also helps to revitalise the food and beverage industry. I believe we should give them business. My grandfather is now working with the cooking staff at a local restaurant. But he always tells me that the number of customers has been gradually decreasing. I assume one of the reasons is that many office workers choose remote work, so they don't visit his restaurant.

To sum up, we should actively visit restaurants to enjoy lunch time. There is great pleasure in eating out and trying different dishes and different restaurants.

▶▶▶ Let's assess the essay:

1. Look at the Appendix A on page 84. Does this sample essay cover the entire checklist? If not, what has not been covered?

_____

_____

_____

_____

2. Look at the rubric on page 7. What marks would you give for the sample writing? Give specific reasons for your rating.

Marks: Format ☐ Language ☐ Message ☐

Reasons: _____

_____

_____

3. Share your marks and reasons with your partner. Discuss with your partner, and arrive at a consensus on the score.

4. What are the positive and negative aspects of this essay? Made suggestions on how to improve it.

_____

_____

_____

_____

4.3 | Writing an argumentative essay

On the basis of your understanding of the rubric indicated on page 7 and the Appendix A on page 84, write your own 280-350-word argumentative essay. Read the following question.

> The United Nations (2022) has been promoting SDGs since 2015 to 'provide a shared blueprint for peace and prosperity for people and the planet, now and into the future' (para 1). Goal 9 aims to 'Build resilient infrastructure, promote inclusive and sustainable industrialization and foster innovation'. To realise this, some companies in developed countries promote building bridges, roads, and railways in developing countries. However, some argue that this may destroy the local environment and ecosystem. Which stance do you support?

The Venn diagram below is useful for writing an argumentative essay. Before writing, let us fill out the diagram.

Body paragraph 1
Evidence:

Opposing viewpoints and refutations:

Introduction
General information or background on the topic
⌄⌄
Thesis statement:

≫

Body paragraph 2
Evidence:

Opposing viewpoints and refutations:

≫

Conclusion

Body paragraph 3
Evidence:

Opposing viewpoints and refutations:

When you have finished writing your essay, try to assess your writing using a checklist on page 84 and rubric indicated on page 7. Next, exchange your writing with your classmates (a minimum of three students) and peer-review each other's work.

▶▶▶ Let's assess your classmate's essay:

1. Look at the Appendix A on page 84. Does your classmate's essay cover the checklist? If not, what has not been covered?

_____

_____

_____

_____

2. Look at the rubric on page 7. What marks would you give for your classmate's writing? Give specific reasons for your rating.

Marks: Format ⬜ Language ⬜ Message ⬜

Reasons: _____

_____

_____

3. What are the positive and negative points of your classmate's essay? Make suggestions on how to improve it.

_____

_____

_____

_____

▶▶▶ Grammar for writing

Repeated noun errors

Repeated noun error refers to the unnecessary repetition of the same noun in a series or a list.

For example,

Original: There were five and eleven students in the first group and second group, respectively.

Revision: There were five and eleven students in the first and second groups, respectively.

Ensure vocabulary fits the context.

Although certain words and phrases in English have similar meanings and/or spellings, they are only used in certain contexts and misuse of such vocabulary may distract or confuse the reader, and in some cases, alter the meaning of the sentence. In addition, certain words and phrases are always or very often used together as fixed expressions. It is also important to ensure that the language used is appropriately formal, informal, or semi-formal, depending on the context.

Example
Original:
Did the writer contain several paragraphs?

Revised:
Did the writer include several paragraphs?

Avoid using contractions like I'd, don't, and can't in academic writing.

Contractions are considered informal in academic writing and should preferably be replaced with their full forms. For example, I'd, don't, and can't should be written as 'I would', 'do not', and 'cannot'.

Example
Avoid: 'Let's reflect on your relationships with…'
Better: 'Let us reflect on your relationships with…'

Maintain a formal tone in academic writing.

In academic writing, words that lend a more formal tone to the sentence are preferred. Therefore, even if the usage is grammatical, words like 'so' at the beginning of a sentence are replaced by 'therefore'.

▶▶▶ Reflection

1. How has this part of learning helped with writing your argumentative essay?

_____

_____

2. What is easy and what is difficult about applying the essence of an argumentative essay to your writing?

_____

_____

3. You have learnt about the application of the argumentative essay to the academic realm. How much can you apply this learning to other subject areas or social life?

_____

_____

_____

_____

Appendix A Check List for Writing

テキストジャンル別のFormatチェックリスト

Part 1. │ 説得型スピーチ原稿

☐ 聞き手 (audience) がどのような人たちか、目的は何かを意識して書いているか。

☐ Ethos, logos, pathosといったrhetoric devicesを取り入れているか。

☐ 話し手の主張が理由や事例、根拠とともに記述されているか。

☐ 聞き手 (audience) にとって分かりやすい言葉を選んで使用しているか。

Part 2. │ ブログ記事

☐ 記事の目的 (アドバイスを行う、事実の伝達をする等) が動詞の命令形や誘い・提案を行う際の表現を用いるなどして (例：Here is my suggestion: , Why don't you…?) 、明確に述べられれているか。

☐ 個人的な経験や体験が記事の内容と関連付けて述べられているか。

☐ 世の中の関心事が、最近の情報とともに述べられているか。

☐ 情報提供に終始するだけでなく、個人的な感想や意見が述べられているか。

☐ 具体的な事例に触れているか。

Part 3. │ フォーマルな電子メール

☐ 宛て名が敬称 (Dear Mr./Ms., To whom it may concern, etc.) とともに書かれているか。

☐ 冒頭に送信の目的が示されているか。

☐ 伝えたい内容が簡潔かつ明確に述べられているか。

☐ 読み手にしてもらいたいことが、丁寧な命令表現で書かれているか (例　I would be appreciated if you could…等)

☐ 送り手の名前が挨拶の文句 (Sincerely, Best regards, 等) とともに示されているか。

Part 4. │ 論説文

☐ 序論・本論・結論の構成になっているか。

☐ 序論にトピックの背景とthesis statement (最も主張したいこと) が記載されているか。

☐ 本論に理由が論拠 (anecdotes (体験や経験) またはevidence (根拠)) とともに示されているか。

☐ 本論で反論を想定し、それに対して反ばくしているか。

☐ 結論では、本論で述べた内容を簡潔にまとめて、かつ序論で述べたthesis statementが言い換えられて (パラフレーズされて) 述べられているか。

☐ 文章全体に一貫性があるか。

Appendix B Peer Review Checklist for Writing

Peer Evaluation

After writing your essay, exchange your writing with your classmates. Use the checklist below to provide your feedback. Please note that your comments should be supportive, analytical and you should also give advice on how your classmates can improve their writing.

1. Format

Did the writer…

- ☐ include several paragraphs?
- ☐ include three to ten sentences in each paragraph?
- ☐ indent the beginning of each paragraph (British style) or insert one line between each paragraph (American style)?
- ☐ use appropriate punctuation: use single quotation marks to indicate a quotation or dialogue (British style) or use double quotation marks to indicate them (American style)?
- ☐ put commas and periods outside the quotation marks (British style), or inside them (American style)?

  For example: Jason claims 'critical thinking is an essential skill'. (British)

  Jason claims "critical thinking is an essential skill." (American)
- ☐ construct an essay with the introduction, body, and conclusion?

2. Languages

Did the writer…

- ☐ use the singular or plural forms correctly?
- ☐ use tenses accurately?
- ☐ try to avoid redundant* expressions?
- ☐ use a lower-case letter after comma and hyphen?

*redundant 冗長な

3. Contents

See the check lists in **Appendix A**.

Integrated English for Critical Thinking
クリティカルシンキングのための総合英語

2023 年 1 月 10 日　初版第 1 刷発行

著　　者　　赤塚祐哉

発 行 者　　森　信久
発 行 所　　株式会社　松 柏 社
　　　　　　〒102-0072　東京都千代田区飯田橋 1 − 6 − 1
　　　　　　TEL　03（3230）4813（代表）
　　　　　　FAX　03（3230）4857
　　　　　　http://www.shohakusha.com
　　　　　　e-mail: info@shohakusha.com

装　　幀　　小島トシノブ（NONdesign）
本文レイアウト・組版　株式会社インターブックス
印刷・製本　　シナノ書籍印刷株式会社
英文校閲　　カクタス・コミュニケーションズ株式会社

ISBN978-4-88198-786-5
略号 = 786
Copyright © 2023 Yuya Akatsuka